BEFORE YOU KNOW YOUR FATE

Poems

Neal Stayton Pratt

Copyright © 2019 by Neal Pratt. All rights reserved.
ISBN 978-1-73436-611-2

Neal Pratt Publishing
Printed in the United States of America

Cover Art by Owen Pratt
Design & Layout by Owen Pratt

Also by Neal Stayton Pratt

SIGHTS & RECOLLECTIONS

THIS PAGE INTENTIONALLY LEFT BLANK

MEANING OF NUMBERS

THE AWFUL WAITING

EVERYTHING LOOKS PRETTIER UNDER CANDLELIGHT

IT'S BEEN A LONG UGLY WINTER

YOU CAN'T PROGRESS WITHOUT A FEW CALLUSES

FIRST DAY OF SPRING

DC DAYS

for Patricia

POEMS

Orange Hate	09	An Audibal Release of Your Soul	43
Mahjong Monday	10	You Are Not There	44
Houston Bound #115	11	April 27th	45
Harvey	12	Mother's Day	46
Hypocrite	13	But Then I Remembered	47
53 Days	14	Could I be the One?	48
But When is Enough?	15	I Could Shed a Tear	49
Holidays in Hospitals	16	Energy Part I	51
Hospital Notes	17	Energy Part II	52
Morphine Dreams	18	Energy Part III	53
I Should Be	19	Happy 95th	54
Waiting	20	Another Page Down	55
I Want to Weep Aloud	21	I Found a Photo	56
A Whisper in Your Ear	22	A Fake Story of a Real Life	57
Will You Leave When I Do?	23	Maybe I Will Miss You	58
I Knew I Lost You	24	I Thought I Lost It	59
Slippers	25	I Think of You	60
Emotional Release	26	Is It Constant?	61
Motherless	27	Was it Worth it?	62
A Great Person to Meet	28	Nothing has Changed	63
The Words Will Remain	29	November 27th	64
Don't Waste the Hours	30	December 3rd	65
Empty Nest	31	December 8th	66
Snow Covered Crevices	32	Soft Light for Seconds	67
Your Mother's Creation	33	Music Boxes	68
I'm Lost	34	So Many Squares	69
Click Click	35	Under Cellophane Spheres	70
Days of the Week	36	You Never Knew Me	71
Last Gasps	37	Compadre Espandro	72
I'm on Autopilot	38	Lake Tahoe for Her	73
Southern Drawl	39	The Energy in Between	75
Shiny Black Cars	40	A Letter of Lost Love	76
Soul Hangs on the Brain	41	The First Real Day of Fall	77
Your Fate is Sealed	42	Photos & Light	78
		Praises of Your Past	79

BEFORE YOU KNOW YOUR FATE

Poems

ORANGE HATE

Some strange things happen
When the crisp seal is cracked open,
Folded over
Exposing clean white lines
Begging to be stained by
Blue fragmented furry, forming phrases.

Maybe it's the cool night air
Humming in swelled temples,
A virtual memory of fireworks displays
Exploding balls of green envy
Orange hate
Red blood
Blue love
Pretty as pumpkin patches in the Fall.

We celebrate seasons and cycles
Rebirth again
Again
Again
Bless these blank pages
And praise the prose
Golden word
Special phrase.

What could it be that keeps the keys
Hidden double breasted?
It's just a stress test
To my wordsmith
With love and devotion
Throughout all the commotion.

MAHJONG MONDAY

They found lesions on your brain
After you seized stiff
On Mahjong Monday.

Now they radiate your skull
Driving the tumors
Back to your abdomen.

I contemplate a plane ride
To see your condition,
But no more than a day or two.

A month of waiting for the results
Before you know your fate,
Or if any of it was worth it.

HOUSTON BOUND #115

I could speak of the dread deep in my heart,
But I get lost in levels and can't find my way.

A 2-ton ball of guilt I drag behind
That she chained around my tiny ankle.

Houston bound and uptown rental car and go
Round the hedges conversing on the phone.

Stroking his beard and waving me in with his right
Past the dead leaves and webs on lights.

Open the creaking door wide
Bald head turning and smile.

Medications stacked in labeled days
Counted and measured through the stages.

Alarms remind through various tones
Times to medicate her bones.

HARVEY

It wasn't until a couple of days before
When they took you seriously
Forecasting future flooding with furry.

We watch from afar on flat TVs
And focus on predicted paths
Praying in vain for protected families.

The canals rapidly rise to roads
Forming flowing river rapids
Rain drains away neighborhoods.

Elderly up to elbows in wading water
Vacated vehicles act as alligators
Floating on flooded freeways.

Houston hopes halted in abandoned apartments
Patiently pleading for rapid rescue
Anxious animals get shoulder carries.

Babies bundled, battling rising waters
As fan boats flee to the scene
Sewing safety for maternal minds.

Water replaces roads with rivers,
Boats busy as bees as families flee,
Homeless heading for safer shelters.

HYPOCRITE

As thousands fled their homes
You closed your doors.

Searching for shelter and food,
You closed the blinds.

Preacher of God
Preacher of sin
Shelter for tax exemption in the end.

You claim flooding from within
With "closed" taped to damp glass.

Seek shelter somewhere else Jesus,
Unless you've brought your cash.

53 Days Left

53 days left in the year,
And I can't get past the fact
That you will leave on one of them.

After all the surgeries,
All the tumors and chemo,
Pain and radiation

Endured for the past 30 years,
I'm amazed you've lasted this long.

I wouldn't call you a fighter,
But most certainly stubborn,
Always set in your ways,

And against all change
That you can't control.

Now you can't control your body
That slowly suffocates your soul
Until one day

One square, marked with a white chalk number
In the upper right corner.
You will be erased with the New Year.

BUT WHEN IS ENOUGH?

November chills spread over dry skin.
A familiar melancholy hits eardrums,

Taking thoughts to hospital beds that
Hug your holiday seasons.

Fluid drains through tangled tubes
As favorite photos are retouched to share.

You lay there dying
Keeping up the fight for family's sake,

But when is enough?
So many topics to discuss

That no one dares to whisper,
Hoping for a speedy recovery.

We patiently await funeral plans and updates,
Looking for someone to take the helm in the storm.

Holidays in Hospitals

I'm trying to remember a date,
A place in time

A moment
A split second,

But left exhausted and guilted
Like when I was a 12-year-old telephone,
Absorbing the back and forth blows.

Some moments of happiness
Not overshadowed by grief,
But all escape my memory,
Leaving me sad for you.

Sad that you lay, propped up on hospital pillows,
Void of happy thoughts of sons.

So many holidays in hospitals,
We confuse the tubes and breathing machines
For tightly wrapped presents.

Monitors beep and patients groan
To the invasions at night.

HOSPITAL NOTES

The hissing of the oxygen mask
And beeping monitors
Offer a carnival of sounds

That entertain my sleepy eyes
Until late night visits
That sound the creaky door.

I sit erect with sweaty back from the stiff chair
That doubles as an uncomfortable bed,
And take shorthand for the morning's brief.

Your face looks like your dad's,
weathered and discolored,
with your mother's frail hands.

Morphine dreams until 9:30
When shades are drawn
Exposing the hazy Houston morning.

MORPHINE DREAMS

6 am morphine shot,
As the sun slips through the shutters
Left ajar from the day before.

Open mouth breathing
Leaves lips longing for moisture
As you lie still, looking like your father in his last days.

Breathing slows while you battle through.
A gasp disturbs the silence as I look
For movement in your chest

That wanes with the minutes that move
Around the red-faced clock, hiding between evergreens
And poinsettias that frame family photos.

Purple blotches stain your cramped hands
That seem to know what is ahead.
Hair follicles poke through in vain

Greeting the holiday pillow case,
Made by the night nurses
That hugs your bald head.

I Should Be

I should be buying a holiday tree,
But instead I'll fly to see you.

I should be hanging lights,
But instead I'll hang my head.

I should be writing holiday cards,
But instead I fill these pages.

I should be planning my weeks ahead,
But instead I'll attend your bedside.

I should be throwing you a birthday party,
But instead I'll plan your funeral.

I should be listening to carols harmonizing in the cold air,
But instead I hear the hiss of the oxygen, puffing your cheeks.

I should be asking you for Xmas wishes,
But instead I'll observe your last words.

I should be filled with holiday joy,
But instead it's only sadness.

I should be prepping family feasts,
But instead I'm prepping deathly details.

I should be catching up on my reading,
But instead I'll edit your obituary.

I should be recalling all the loving memories,
But instead I draw a blank.

I should be kissing you hello,
But instead I'll kiss you goodbye.

WAITING

Waiting for the minute hand to click
Waiting for my eyes to close from exhaustion
Waiting for your breaths to slow to a stop
Waiting for your last gasp before your body gives in
Waiting for your eyes to open, with their new haze
Waiting for the nurses to come with soothing shots
Waiting for your organs to give up the fight
Waiting for your pain to cease
Waiting for families to forgive
Waiting for funeral calls
Waiting for the floods to stop
Waiting for my blue pilot to dry up
Waiting for clean clothes and soft sheets
Waiting for vital signs to drop
Waiting for my mind to rest
Waiting for my emotions to take hold
Waiting for the memories to come
Waiting for the sweet return
Waiting for the skin to chill
Waiting for your love to wane
Waiting for your disease to run its course
Waiting for your hands to relax
Waiting for your head to fall
Waiting for the photos to be removed
Waiting for the balloons to deflate
Waiting for the last words that already came
Waiting for the mother and child reunion
Waiting for the waiting to end as you labor through your death.

I Want to Weep Aloud

Funeral arrangements are made on rainy days
As you labor with slow breaths,
Gasping for more memories to unfold.

Siblings whisper sweet sayings in your ear,
As you struggle to hear
Flickering your hazy eyes.

Guests come and go at intervals
As you sleep through the days
Preparing for your return.

I try to capture a memory
As you lay, looking like your father
From 20 years earlier.

I want to weep aloud
As you sleep soundly,
But I can't find the feelings.

A Whisper in Your Ear

A soft hand on your bald head
That sprouts tiny greys from the
Break in chemo treatments.

A whisper in your ear
To let you know I'm here,
And you are not alone.

Dry eyes and a broken heart
Staring at your stillness
Waiting to be turned.

Vitals are checked and logged
Giving indication of where you are
Along your labored journey.

Wet sponge to your dry lips
From the oxygen and morphine
And gaping frowned mouth.

Blotched cold skin
From the blood slowing
and stopping short.

A shell slowly letting go
Through gasps of air
And weakened pulse.

WILL YOU LEAVE WHEN I DO?

Could this be the last?

The last night seeing you alive?

Midafternoon flight tomorrow,

But will you live another visit?

The congestion in your chest says otherwise.

Phlegm in your throat,

But you're too weak to expel

With your elevated head.

Will you leave when I do?

The awful waiting shakes my sweaty bones,

Sore from lack of slumber.

The rattling racket within your chest

Moves my tortured soul

With every exhale.

I Knew I Lost You

I knew it was you before I even looked at my phone.

I knew the words that you say.

I knew the way my heartbeat would increase with the ring.

I knew this day would come.

I knew your body would give before your spirit.

I knew I would be the last to know.

I knew the tears would come.

I knew you were on borrowed time.

I knew I lost you long ago.

I knew I would never hear your voice again.

I knew you had said your last word.

I knew the pain was finally finished.

I knew my heart would break.

I knew I was truly motherless for the first time.

I knew the future was uncertain.

I knew when your spirit left,

And dropped first flakes of winter that kissed

the cold pavement.

SLIPPERS

Slippers peeking out from the darkness of the bed,
Subtly suggesting warm toes with bathroom visits,
But those days have past,
Leaving the slippers as lonely as my heart.

EMOTIONAL RELEASE

I wait for it to come,
For the tears to flow freely.

My ducts are dry,
Arid like the Texas winds

That blow me into the concrete streets,
Still wet from Harvey.

I want to scream and yell,
But just sit and stare,

A motionless speck on the worn
Upholstered sofa cushion.

MOTHERLESS

No matter how you pretend
Or what you say to your friends,
It's different when it actually happens.

Gold badge membership
Without the perks,
Without the hassle.

Take a ticket, and stand in line
Advice is waiting around the corner
Third window on your left.

You should be used to the isolation,
Or at least more prepared
For the lack of words to come.

Now you're saved in children stories
To be ingrained in their memories
While your face is lost in my dreams.

A Great Person to Meet

The words from the pamphlet described her as someone who'd
I'd love to meet.

A slide show of photos
Flashes behind a photo of you from twenty years ago.

Vacations and milestones fade in and out
Showing smiles from the past.

The sons even make an appearance,
Maybe 4 or five, all before 25 years old.

The religious figure in front
Highlighted her smile, kindness, and friendship.

She declared you, "A great person to be around,"
And I thought, "I would like to meet this person."

Surely this can't be the same woman
That chose her new husband over her kids

That went years without speaking
That informed me I was the cause of her ruined life.

She was in no hurry to have a relationship with her grandkids,
At least the ones with her blood.

I Heard my mother being eulogized
And realized I didn't know her

And she didn't know me,
And felt like an outsider at your funeral

Far from the front row reserved for family.
Two different people.

To them she was…
To me she was…

THE WORDS WILL REMAIN

My notebook is falling apart
Teaching me a lesson on impermanence.

You lasted 68 years and 11 days,
Longer than my notebook could ever promise.

The binding fails as the blue ink fades
Into unreadable scribble.

The words will remain until burned
Into the pyre fire, like your soulless body

Waiting for the weight of ashes
To be poured in the urn

That will decorate a mantle
Until the frozen lake thaws, and his body turns cold.

DON'T WASTE THE HOURS

Don't let these days go by
Lost in routine

Don't waste the hours
For perfect moments to reflect.

The memories will be gone by that time,
With nothing to show for it.

Fill the lines with colorful reflections
And lament over missed opportunities.

EMPTY NEST

Boned chilled darkness
Heavy on layered legs

Holiday lights illuminate the blinds
Sending haloed glows floating into the room.

Holiday season has sizzled
Along with visiting plans.

What may come of the visits?
Is it just symbolic?

Father and son
Spiritual guest
Empty nest.

Your nest was emptied years ago,
Barren branches blowing in the breeze.

Silent pianos lie dormant in corners
Awaiting to be dragged away

Through green mountains and salty turnpikes
that wind through slopped hillsides.

Cold air stings clogged nostrils from frigid freeze
Arid from the arctic air.

SNOW COVERED CREVICES

Snow covered crevices
Hugging frozen rivers
Cut into hillsides
30 thousand feet below.

Grids planned long ago
Plotted pastures
Lying dormant
Beneath the freeze.

Smoke trails paint the think air
Dodging streaks
Criss-crossing
The vast horizon.

Dots come together forming factories
That spit cities
From smoke stacks

Trees stand tall
Protecting perfect parcels
Shadowed by the white
Of winter's kiss.

YOUR MOTHER'S CREATION

You never got your family,
The family you always longed for.

Your matriarch dreams damaged
By severed love

Lost to the sea and city
Where winds blow guilt from frozen lakes.

You wanted to replicate
Your mother's creation

Without the effort
Or affection.

Reward without work
Left you estranged

And left us empty
Roaming cities with heavy shoulders.

I'M LOST

Green door narrow hallways
Open mournful souls that remember
Day
By
Day
Cathartic awakenings
On door knockers
That greet hallway dwellers.
I'm lost
Wondering the city
Dreaming of psychic advise
If it doesn't bring you joy
You must let her go.

CLICK CLICK

Snowy morning drive
Dodging parked cars
And head-on collisions
From a congested D St.

Ring ring on my phone.
I see his name,
And I already know the reason
for the morning call.

She past as the snow
Drifted down below
Through the orange glow
Of the street light.

I pull over to the curb
To hear the news.
People passing
Flashers flashing.

Click click
They cycle on and off
Soothing my soul
With the touch of her hand.

DAYS OF THE WEEK

I said "good morning" on Tuesday,
And was shocked from your
"good morning" reply so clear.

I heard you died on Friday
Sending silent snow
That blurred my dreams.

It was on Thanksgiving Thursday
Reminding me of your mother
With last words over the phone.

You never spoke on Saturday
When Helen hovered over you
Remembering all the past years.

It was silent all-day Sunday
Sounding Edith Piaf
Stroking your stumbled head.

I cancelled my flight on Monday
Fearing the failing
Of your labored breathing.

LAST GASPS

I wasn't there
When you had your last breath.

Friday drinking and smoking
Sleeping in under covers drawn.

Night sweats with one leg hanging out to catch the wind
That circle throughout the room.

You with your morphine dreams
Saying "good morning" long after you past.

I saw you gasp on Tuesday
Sending chills down my spine.

Cradling your head
With false words of assurance.

But you lasted three more days,
Always persistent; a trait that drove us apart.

I'm on Autopilot

Sunrise comes through
Six paned windows

Awakening shadows that stretch
Across the stained wood floors

I'm on autopilot
Spiraling down
While routines abound

SOUTHERN DRAWL

Southern drawl
And amazing smile
It's hard to imagine
You're nothing but ashes.

Cropped hair with bangs
In early business portraits
It's hard to believe
You're just a photo.

Gold necklace
From your mother's ring
It's hard to fathom
You're living on the mantle.

High cheek bones
With smooth skin
Now melted away
Along with my memory.

Shiny Black Cars

Shiny black cars
Are wiped down
And lined end to end.

They wait in silence
As black suits talk temperatures
Until the time strikes.

Widows are walked
To tinted windows
That black out the sorrow.

The blooming blossoms of the tulips
Beckon for Spring and soak in the sun
And the last wisps of wind.

SOUL HANGS ON THE BRAIN

Hands holding frail bones
Sunken cheeks and shortened breath.

Moment by moment
Clinging to the past

Sliver of opportunity
15 minutes in the tunnel.

Delusions of conceptual structures
Out through nonconscious space

Ever expanding beyond the past
Soul hangs on the brain.

Not the heart
Just a bad metaphor

Letting go willingly
But at your own pace.

YOU FATE IS SEALED

Early morning light
Seeps past the rain drops and open blinds
Creating a mirror image
On the glossy gray granite island top.

Sounds of water boiling excites my coffee grounds
To calm my mind and alter my focus
Away from your oxygen mask
And empty room.

Waiting for us to come rescue you.
Your fate is sealed without your knowledge
Hidden in raindrops that gather
As your water dish sits empty.

An Audibal Release of Your Soul

I drink my coffee
And read the news
As you lie with oxygen tubes
And heavy panting.

Ominous drive to the hospital
Rewinding turns our attention to the wolves
As thoughts of our white wolf flash with memories.

We bring your blanket to the family room
And wait for the awful inevitable.
Paperwork is completed with crisp signatures,
Signing your life away.

We hug your white fur
And cry out longings for more time.
Shots are given and breathing slows,
As the process is explained to youthful minds.

Heart stops with your eyes open
As the last air in your lungs
Is released through your still jowls
In an audible release of your soul.

Tiny tears rain down
Wetting the white fur lying motionless
On your blue blanket
Tattered with tears.

YOU ARE NOT THERE

I walk back into the room
Expecting to find you curled up
Shrimp-like: feet against the wall
Head upside down,
Acknowledging my presence
before diverting your eyes back to the wall.
But you are not there,
Only matted carpet that collected hair,
Almost in an outline of your body.
You went from a 2-year-old to a 12-year-old in a few weeks,
Astonished at the rapid pace of digression,
Playing out in real time.
Languished eyes and protruding bones
Under white fur lying motionless
On hardwood with heavy breathing
And quickened heartbeats.

APRIL 27TH

When you think about it, euthanasia is better
Than watching a loved one slowly decay

Until their body gives up and fades away.
I'd rather give the shot to her, to avoid the
Long nights of suffering to breathe.

2 am phone calls:
The fluid is building up around the lungs
With shallow heavy breathing,

Struggling for air,
Slowly suffocating.

Saddened eyes as you starred into my soul
And knew your time was up.

MOTHER'S DAY

This was my first without you,
Although it feels the same
As when you were alive and silent
A thousand miles away.

Almost as I'm looking
Through the day behind frosted glass
That skews the reality
That you are not here.

We celebrated her with flowers
And homemade cards that glisten
With colored glue that glows
In uneven sprinkles.

The day has a new definition
A new focus of the lens
I toss the frosted glass behind
And focus on the future.

We walk with her through the gardens
That wind through the willows
Leaving your memory in the Marigolds
To sprout with the Spring Tulips.

BUT THEN I REMEMBERED

I almost called you yesterday
To wish your voicemail a Happy Mother's Day,
But then I remembered.

I was going to have daisies
Delivered to your apartment,
But then I remembered.

I remembered your last gasps
As your lungs labored
While your heart had other plans.

I remembered your last words,
"Good morning;" almost reflexive,
Awakening from your death slumber.

I remembered that you were
Never really there
When you were awake.

I almost called you yesterday
To wish your voicemail a Happy Mother's Day,
But then I remembered.

COULD I BE THE ONE?

Could I be the one
To scribble down the memories
From distorted minds,
As sweat slides down my back?

Could I make it rhyme
Like all those greats
Who held accolades
At such early age?

Could I write it down
Before my hand sticks
To the page
With sweaty dew?

How many times can
I rearrange the words
In your favor before
The heat melts my memories?

I Could Shed a Tear

I could shed a tear
At just the thought

Of looking down
On dirty bangs

With innocent smiles
That rise to the cheekbones.

I could shed a tear
At just the thought

Of imagining
the stitched shoes are switched

And we are driven
To disastrous decisions.

I could shed a tear
At just the thought

Of being stripped away
From huggable hands.

Terror in her eyes
How they terrorize.

I could shed a tear
At just the thought

Of kept concealed
In cramped cages

Faded families
With foiled faces.

I could shed a tear
At just the thought

Of little lungs
Expressing longing

For maternal bosom
Now broken within.

I could shed a tear
At just the thought

Of scared sisters sobbing
Hysterically huddled and alone.

I could shed a tear
At just the thought.

ENERGY PART I

If you are energy
In your new form,
How do you separate yourself
From other energies?

Do you still have memories,
Or did you leave those behind
In the ash?

Have you tried to communicate with us?
Perhaps hacked into our network
To leave goodbyes not said?

You never did when you were living,
So why should you start now?

Heaven has call waiting,
But I still get your busy signal,
Broken relationships over bad connections.

ENERGY PART II

I thought I felt your energy today,

But it could have been just memories,

Dangling

Shimmering

To catch the first light

Reflected from front windows.

Odd feelings

Arise tense muscles

And apathy

That shut down like a child

Because in the end,

It doesn't really matter.

ENERGY PART III

You come slipping out
Of white pages that send lines
in perfect parallels that transmit
gentle reminders of your energy

Black knuckle punch
Stirs my skipping memory
Reminding me of missions
Abandoned, from dried up resources

Hanging like a mobile
For small fingers to fan
As they gleefully grasp
For the chaotic spinning

Until calming like a river
When the bed stones appear
To capture the thoughts
Of cheekbone smiles that now rest in the darkness

HAPPY 95TH

Your youngest called me today
To remind me of your birth-95 years ago,

Some state in 1923 where
You cried your first breath.

You breathed your last breath
In Shreveport, 1999.

I watched your body
Lowered in the hole-perfectly rectangle

And watched how she shed
Her diamond tears perfectly

Running down her cheeks,
That have now turned to ash,

And sitting on a mantle between
Tax files from 1997 and Dick Francis novels.

ANOTHER PAGE DOWN

Another page down
In my homage to you,
A pedestal you never had.

Middle child
Only girl
Spoiled in your brothers' opinions.

You battled through divorce
And quickly picked up the pieces
Left shattered like broken trusts.

You couldn't make ends meet
And sold us down the river
And then guilted us for our absence.

I erect a statue in honor
Of your suffering not discussed,
Dismissed under dinner napkins

And laid to rest with your ashes
That stay quiet in the dark urn
That holds your forgotten dreams.

I Found a Photo

I found a photo of you
1970
Of you and dad.

You're wearing a mid-thigh dress
1969
With cropped hair.

Fence line backdrop
At a relative's wedding
Whose name has faded with the photo.

Ruston, LA stories abound
After wine and gin are poured
Under the dim lights of NC.

Right arm around your waist
A security blanket you cherished
Before your love died.

A FAKE STORY OF A REAL LIFE

I just reread your obituary
And wanted to express my thoughts
In red ink on the margins:

A fake story of a real life,
Fabricated to sever heated wounds,
Exposing the tissue to December air.

A better version was scrapped
Because the tip wasn't sharp enough
To draw common blood.

No input needed to tell her story,
Omitting two decades until you came,
Riding on your halo, just above our heads.

Birth orders are rearranged
To align with your family tree,
Painted in your linear mind.

I just reread your obituary
And am still nauseous with disgust
And wondering where I fit in now.

MAYBE I WILL MISS YOU

Maybe I let you down,
Down in the Texas heat
That hovers over asphalt
And mixes with the smog.

Maybe I didn't live
Up to your expectations
That hung just over my head
And taint my thoughts.

Maybe I was stubborn,
Unwilling to bend
To rules that held down
Smothering ambition.

Maybe I'm just like you,
Always thinking of myself
From one-sided views
That dominate the conversation.

Maybe I will miss you
When my heart finally breaks
And falls through wrinkled fingers
Curled with death.

I Thought I Lost It

I thought I lost it when I lost you,
That guilt that hangs so heavy,
A cloud that blankets the sun's shadows.

Now it arises again
Scarring temples with memories
Of crying cheeks and dirty hands, looking to be held.

I Think of You

I think of you
On sunny days
Where the chill runs across my toes
And the rays are bright.

I think of you
As Fall appears
Counting down the days until your anniversary
Of your hospital trip.

I think of you as birthdays gather
Waiting to be celebrated with streamers and wine
And overdue cards in the mail.

I think of you
As the traffic sounds
Through the rustling of the dry leaves
That carry in the wind.

I think of you
As I sit silently
Playing the last moments in my heads,
Like a spinning record.

Is it Constant?

I wonder how time exists
When you're nothing but energy
Floating between thought bubbles.

Are hours minutes or
Years seconds?

Is it constant?

It's almost been a year for me
Since you checked in and never left.

How have you spent your time?
I hope you're socializing with others.

Was It Worth It?

Was it worth it?
I have to ask myself
As I reflect on the past,
Four decades worth.

I can't imagine that it was,
Considering what you had
Before you left it all
To pursue new feelings.

New love
Through channels
Close to home.

Was it worth it,
To lose your family,
Parents, siblings, and kids,
Sacrificing relationships for your guilt?

The guilt that you passed down
Like a baton, but without the encouragement.

Was it worth it
To be alone, together
For the last thirty years
Alienating everyone you can't control?

Was it worth all the stress
That slowly destroyed your
Insides from the day you said, "I do"?

Was it worth it to end
Up gasping for air in your final moments
As siblings give goodbye kisses on your bald head
As you slip into the morning snowfall?

NOTHING HAS CHANGED

My first birthday without her,
But really nothing has changed.

When she did call, which wasn't often,
She'd remind me that it wouldn't be official until 10:48pm.

The woman who carried and birthed me
Is not here to reminisce of long ago times.

No more day after voicemails left on phones
Sitting dormant during slumber.

I went to see you this time last year
When you were able to speak, although we didn't speak.

Not of important topics,
The air was too cluttered with guilt and false hope.

You only said there was no money,
That you left everything to the hospital.

No end of life admissions or advice to eager ears,
Just useless small talk between morphine drips

That waste precious time with distorted dreams
That ease your insides toward failure.

Now I sit in silence
Reflecting on my everything owed to her.

My first birthday without her,
But really nothing has changed.

NOVEMBER 27TH

You would have turned 69 today,
But your body gave out just after
The candles were extinguished last year,
With one final birthday wish.

We celebrated her birthday with donuts and hot chocolate,
And as she blew the flames, I thought of you,
And how you cherished this shared day
Between the generations.

She was always your favorite
Because of your common date,
But she has forgotten within the year,
As most 10-year olds do.

She unwrapped her gifts
With her great smile
As I watched in awe
And thought of you on your 69th birthday.

December 3rd

I skipped her last birthday to be with you.
Now she is a year older and you are gone.

I wished her a happy birthday over the phone,
Sitting on stiff sofas that absorb grief.

For a minute, I thought about possibilities of you
Being born on one daughter's birthday and dying
On the other's birthday.

Grief takes over and my heart is in two places
As one grows while the other dies.

Smiles turn to death frowns with chapped lips,
Patted wet with cool water sponges slowing the
Shriveling of skin.

DECEMBER 8TH

I counted down the squares
To get to this date.
365 squares that all look the same.

I waited for snowfall
To commensurate the day.
Clouds and cold was all we got.

I waited for your call,
The one I never got,
But always missed.

Your love was all I wanted
Your heartache was all you got.
I had to remind the kids because kids can't recall.

The memories are lost to distraction
Of colored leaves that fall protecting the grass
From the winter snow.

Dinner with in-law's friends
Distract my mind with recipes and cocktails
And smiles so kind.

A square on a board and ash in a jar
With scattered memories,
Is all that you are.

SOFT LIGHT FOR SECONDS

I tried to forget,
But the more I try
The more they appear
In soft light for seconds until fading
Back to the trenches.

I wish we could have made
A few more smiles along the way,
But we took a different path
And stayed the course until we ended up so far away.

Your funeral was a fake,
But it's what you would have wanted
With tears dripping scripture
Singing psalms of sorrow to
Lift your heavy spirit to the heavens
With open arms that always forgive.

MUSIC BOXES

Music box dancer
Tip toes into memories.

I wanted to share it with you,
But ears have become deaf.

No more memories to share
As the generations fade.

Photographs living in
Darkness of unopened boxes.

I shudder to think how many times
We could have talked, but sat in silence.

We could have laughed, but cried

We could have shared, but kept secrets hidden
In ivory and pearl music boxes that dance
With tip toes in dreams.

So Many Squares

So many squares on my calendar,
It's hard to pick a date.

Which number will you give up on?
When your breathing slows
Then stops?

Which day will your eyes close
Never to open again?

They say it's doubtful you'll make the New Year.
I stare at the roulette wheel wondering
Where your last words will land.

Phone calls fill in the gaps
Yet leave trenches in the end.

Hard topics are avoided
Like the relationships we pretended to have.

So many events, the squares are filling up,
Leaving a few blank dates to travel and visit.
Sorting details left in the stacks

Of papers systematically arranged and dated
With Post-It notes and permanent marker.

Could it be my birthday, or yours?
Maybe a grandchild's or New Year's Eve,
celebrating your new life
As the crystal balls and champagne drop?

Under Cellophane Spheres

Balloons and flowers decorate the room,
Bringing celebrations to the dismal scene.

Cards taped to mantles display tiny handprints
And badly spelled words that radiate love without loss.

I watch you labor under cellophane spheres
That dangle colored ribbons that slowly sway

To the life that leaves your body.
Open mouthed frown shows that days are numbered now.

No more conversation, just occasional eye openings,
And then back to morphine dreams.

YOU NEVER KNEW ME

You never really knew me
You only knew my face.

A train on your tracks
Never looking back
You never knew me.

Silent car rides down
Distant Texas roads

Starring out the window
Watching the prairies pass.

COMPADRE ESPANDRO

Follow
Beautiful
Why
Why
Why
Why not?

LAKE TAHOE FOR HER

Three sets of ashes
Stacked neatly on closet floors
Between shoeboxes and sweatshirts.

Blue velvet gathering dust,
Like you,
Now covered in plastic and red oak

Waiting for the perfect place
To lay you down, side by side
Ash and dirt.

Lake Tahoe for her,
Where the cliff and lake meet.

LEAVE ME A COIN

Leave me a coin
A 1976
Year of my birth
To show me you're there.

An aged penny
Centered
Oddly placed
Moved with your magnetism.

THE ENERGY IN BETWEEN

The Blackbirds descend onto the newly cut grass
Chaotically pecking the ground
For the newly-exposed food source.

They rummage before being startled,
Flying up to the power poles
To chirp their discontent.

I wonder where your energy has gone,
Maybe a bird, shuffling for worms in the wind,
Or maybe the energy in between.

Sometimes I sit and wonder.

A Letter of Lost Love

Sometimes I want to write you a letter
To better effectively communicate my reasons
In hopes of explaining,

But then habits take over
And I abandon all thoughts of you,
As if you were still alive.

I did write you a letter once,
Addressed to him, but it was never read
And is likely collecting dust within a file of disappointments.

A letter of lost love,
And where it was lost, and all went wrong
As we both took our own courses.

A letter of forgiveness
For all your wrongs
That shaped the me that angered you.

I'll have you in my memories and will recall you
From time to time to keep the embers glowing
until I burn and our energies can try again.

THE FIRST REAL DAY OF FALL

I'm drawn outside by the clinging
Of the notes emitting from distant ice cream trucks
That calls out the addicts from dark slumbers
To face the first real day of Fall.

Pounding sounds from handy projects
Provide the rhythm to the high-pitched keys
That chime "Home on the Range" to
"Yankee Doodle" to Mozart and back again.

The notes dance in the chilly winds
That shake limbs awake
Testing their endurance until they suddenly stop
And are replaced with siren screams that echo closer
with every wail.

PHOTOS & LIGHT

Pictures of innocent youth
Sixteen sweetheart
With future dreams,
Leans on the stained
Home-made bookshelf
That doubles as a headset.

Perfect smile that holds
Up rosy cheekbones
That glow through the
Black and white gloss

All you are
All you were
And ever will be
Are just photos and light preserved.

PRAISES OF YOUR PAST

Black cars line streets
As flags are flown half-mast.

The flag is carried from Capitol to Cathedral
Somber waves as the motorcade passes.

The bells toll for thee
As heads turn, following the casket past.

Heels go click clack on wooden floors
That echo through stained glass.

Sing exalted all triumphant
As we drown with praises of your past.

www.ingramcontent.com/pod-product-compliance
Lightning Source LLC
Chambersburg PA
CBHW051713040426
42446CB00008B/863